Prophecy of the Russian Epic

*How the Holy Mountains Released
the Mighty Russian Heroes
from their Rocky Caves*

Sergei O. Prokofieff

TEMPLE LODGE
London

Translated from the Russian by Simon Blaxland de Lange

Published by Temple Lodge 1993

Originally published in Russian by Noah Press, Yerevan, Armenia 1992

© 1992 Sergei O. Prokofieff
This translation © 1993 Temple Lodge Publishing

The publishers wish to express their gratitude to Karla Kiniger for working on the translated text

A catalogue record for this book is available from the British Library

ISBN 0 904693 49 X

Cover by S. Gulbekian
Drawing by Gabriella de Carvalho (based on the central motif of the St Michael icon in the Cathedral of the Archangel Michael in the Kremlin, Moscow)
Typeset by DP Photosetting, Aylesbury, Bucks
Printed and bound in Great Britain by
Cromwell Press Limited, Broughton Gifford, Wiltshire

Contents

Foreword

The prophetic Russian epic or bylina *How the Holy Mountains Released the Mighty Russian Heroes from their Rocky Caves* is as regards its character an altogether unique example of Russian folk art. This prophetic bylina was directly inspired from spiritual sources. Hence it is not enough merely to be open to it on an artistic and emotional level; it is necessary to gain a real *understanding* of the *spiritual reality* which was perceived by the Russian seeress who then clothed her vision with the story of the bylina. Only then will this bylina be able to reveal to the reader the full depth of its wisdom and the meaning of its insights, and—like a streak of lightning—illumine the whole historical path of Russia from the past, through the present and into the future.

How is it possible for us today to come closer to an understanding of the supersensible reality behind the images of the bylina? An answer to this question may be found through the modern science of the spirit, Anthroposophy, which presents a Sophian, that is, a cosmic teaching about anthropos, or man.

Founded at the beginning of the 20th century by the Austrian philosopher and spiritual researcher Rudolf Steiner (1861–1925), as a result of his having attained a modern Christian initiation, Anthroposophy enables us to enter into the inner meaning of the Russian bylina, and to understand it in its full spiritual depth and significance.

This is why in the present edition the bylina is offered to the reader in an anthroposophical interpretation. Its text is preceded by a brief introduction into certain anthroposophical concepts, this being followed by a commentary on the bylina which—with the help of these concepts—will enable us to enter into its spiritual content.

Readers wishing to familiarise themselves further with anthroposophical teachings will find at the end of the book a list of the principal works by Rudolf Steiner.

Sergei O. Prokofieff

An Introduction to Certain Concepts
of Anthroposophy

According to the modern science of the spirit (spiritual science), the human being consists not only of the physical body that is visible to the eye but also of higher, supersensible 'bodies', which are discernible only to spiritual consciousness.

Whereas man's physical body gives him a relationship to the mineral world, his next higher—and outwardly imperceptible (supersensible)—body, called in spiritual science the life-body, relates him to the plant world, to everything that has the capacity of growth and propagation. The next, still higher supersensible member of man's being—the soul-body—relates him to the animal world, to everything that can feel and have sensations. At the same time, it represents that part of the human soul which is most connected with the physical body and is strongly dependent on its functions. Finally, the highest supersensible member and true focus of man's being, his holy of holies, is his 'I' or ego—the bearer of individual *self-consciousness*—which fundamentally distinguishes him from the rest of the natural world and makes him a completely independent kingdom of his own, alongside the kingdoms of nature: the mineral, plant and animal worlds. As the possessor of an individual ego, man is truly the 'crown of nature'.

From the ego, the central member of his being, he then achieves the gradual transformation of the three lower members, or bodies, into higher members. At first this work is brought about unconsciously, under the guidance of spiritual beings, and only later, to the extent that individual ego-consciousness awakens within him, does he increasingly begin to accomplish this himself. This process defines the whole cultural-historical evolution of earthly humanity. It unfolds in two stages. First, the work on the three lower members—the soul-, life- and physical bodies—is carried out on a *soul* level and only later, at higher stages of evolution, at a spiritual level.

As a result of the work accomplished at the first stage, the human soul establishes its independence from the physical body and, as an independent soul organisation, acquires a threefold structure. Each of the three soul members is, therefore, the result of the work of the individual ego on the lower bodies and has its particular designation in spiritual science. Thus the soul-body is gradually transformed into the sentient soul, the life-body into the intellectual soul (also called the soul of character), and the physical body into the consciousness soul. Simultaneously with this the ego, in incorporating itself in these three soul members, attains higher stages in its evolution which may be seen essentially as bridges in its conscious development.

To begin with, in the sphere of the sentient soul, the forces of the individual ego are manifested only very dimly. At this stage of his evolution man has not yet fully separated himself from that social environment in which he was originally placed—be it family, race, village or religious community. He is connected with them in his entire being, he lives within their boundaries, assiduously following established customs, habits and traditions. At the same time, it is in the sentient soul that man gains the most direct access to the sources of spiritual and religious powers which, while being able to fill his soul, do not fully reach his consciousness. Hence the name of this soul member, the *sentient soul*, inasmuch as the human ego, in working within it, enters into a relationship with the rest of the world directly through sensation rather than through rational knowledge. All that may be regarded as naive, as being bereft of questions and doubts but with a deep and sincere faith, is characteristic of this member of the soul. In Russian history, the soul configuration of the majority of the peasants until the end of the 19th century, and in some areas until the beginning of the 20th century, corresponds to this state of being.

The manifestation of the ego in the intellectual soul, or soul of character, is associated with the soul mood of people who live in towns and have to a certain degree assimilated the fruits of human culture as a whole. At this stage the human ego begins for the first time to base its relationship to the world on thinking, on the faculty of reason, which greatly hastens the individualisation process within man. Parallel with this, the first features of personal character begin to appear within him with ever greater clarity, and the characterological foundation for all subsequent soul development is formed. Hence this soul member is called the *intellectual soul* or *soul of character*.

Within the boundaries of the intellectual soul, however, the human ego comes to expression in such a way that outer authority, whether it be religious, scientific or of the state, exerts a definite influence upon human life. In this sense the words of St Augustine, 'I would never have come to believe in the Gospels if the authority of the Catholic Church had not forced me to',[1] are a thoroughly characteristic expression of the intellectual soul or soul of character.

Summing up, one can say that, whereas at the first stage we take certain steps without thinking about them, as though instinctively and directly trusting in our inner feeling, at the second stage we begin to be guided by commandments, laws or other rules communicated from without, which strictly regulate our personal lives and social conduct.

Only in the consciousness soul are all the capacities and qualities of the individual ego revealed in their full measure. At this stage of his evolution man seeks to derive the motives for his actions solely out of himself. Now he aspires to extricate himself from all the outer authorities that have in one way or another been foisted upon him, so as to experience himself as a free personality who can determine his own destiny independently and in full consciousness. Henceforth, all his actions stem solely from an inner impulse, rooted in clear knowledge and expressed in a pure love for the deed.

Rudolf Steiner characterised this stage of inner development at some length in his book *The Philosophy of Freedom*, where he defines it as 'ethical individualism'.[2] And this, inasmuch as it is based on the fully conscious activity of the individual ego, can be attained only in the highest soul member, the *consciousness soul*. From what has been said it becomes understandable that it is in the very period when this highest soul member is being developed amongst humanity as a whole that man is particularly subjected to the great temptation of using the freedom that he has gained not for moral purposes but only for the satisfaction of his personal egotism, for an arrogant and self-satisfied contentment with purely outward, material achievements. And yet, if earthly humanity is not to lose the higher meaning of its existence and is to attain at some future time all the goals that the divine rulership of the world has placed before it, there will be a need for it to direct the individual freedom that had been attained in the consciousness soul towards spiritual things. This means working towards the gradual spiritualisation of the consciousness soul, thus opening the way to transforming the lower members of man's being into their higher counterparts not merely at a soul but also at a spiritual level.

Orientating the consciousness soul towards moral and spiritual goals as a basis for all subsequent spiritual work is one of the central tasks of Anthroposophy in our time. For the principal power that is available to the human ego in the consciousness soul is the yearning for knowledge. One of its aspects is knowledge of the material world. But Anthroposophy opens up another aspect—knowledge of the supersensible world, whence its entire development is directed towards the spirit.

As a result of this work of the ego on the spiritual plane, man's spirit is eventually also to acquire a threefold structure, thereby bringing about an awakening to higher spiritual knowledge. Thus the fully transformed soul-body is eventually to become the bearer of what spiritual science calls the *Spirit-Self*, or the spirit which works within the ego and, from there, spiritualises the entire soul-body as the most immediate sphere of its influence. Subsequently, the fully transformed life-body will become the bearer of what spiritual science calls the *Life-Spirit*, that is, a spirit which is able to spiritualise man's life-body. Finally, spiritual work on the physical body will lead in future to its being permeated by the highest spirituality. The stage of development that is attained in this way is in spiritual science called that of *Spirit-Man*, inasmuch as its result is the spiritualisation of man in his entirety.[3]

Of course, the attainment of this high purpose is not possible during one short earthly life but only in the course of a series of incarnations. Hence the truth of reincarnation is a highly important part of the modern science of the spirit.[4] However, it radically differs in this respect from the teachings of the East, where the idea of reincarnation is presented as an endless cycle of births and deaths, without beginning or end; and, moreover, it has nothing in common with fanciful notions about the transmigration of souls.

From the standpoint of spiritual science, the process of reincarnation in the evolution of the world and of humanity has quite definite bounds. Its beginning is associated with that event which is characterised at the beginning of the Bible as 'the Fall' (Genesis ch. 3), and it will finally come to an end in that distant epoch of *universal spiritualisation* described at the end of the Revelation of St John (ch. 20–21). It follows from this that the work of man's spiritualisation will at the same time be associated with the process of the liberation and transformation of the whole world, of 'all creation'. For to the extent that his soul-body is spiritualised, the possibility opens up before man of working on the gradual spiritualisation of the animal kingdom; in the process of spiritualising his life-body he will be able to begin working on the plant kingdom; and finally, with the transformation of his physical body will come the possibility of reaching towards the spiritualisation of the mineral kingdom.

It is in this sense that we should understand the words of Paul the Apostle, that 'all creation has been groaning and travailing together until now' (Romans 8: 22) awaiting its liberation from bondage (v. 21), which can come only from human individuals who have embarked upon the path of the conscious spiritualisation of their being. And this, according to Paul, is possible only if they become 'sons of God' (v. 19), through the permeation of each human individual with the 'Spirit of Christ'(v. 9).

These utterances of the Apostle Paul are fully confirmed by Anthroposophy, which derives its knowledge from the sources of modern spiritual research. And amongst the most important of its results is the knowledge of the direct participation of Christ in the whole evolutionary process that has been characterised. For since His union with Earth existence through passing through death on the Hill of Golgotha and His Resurrection, Christ has become the

7

chief helper of each individual ego in its work of spiritualising the being of man and, through it, the whole earthly world.

Thus from the standpoint of spiritual science it is necessary to acknowledge that the process of the spiritualisation of man and the world would have been altogether impossible without Christ's union with earthly evolution as its higher archetype and ultimate goal. And the words of Christ Himself, 'Lo, I am with you always, until the closing of the age' (Matthew 28: 20), testify to this. Therefore the work of the steady spiritualisation of man is at the same time the process of the gradual 'enchristening' of the human individual—and potentially of the whole of humanity—through his permeation by the Christ Spirit, which is revealed in the human spirit as a trinity (Spirit-Self, Life-Spirit and Spirit-Man), as the microcosmic reflection in him of the Holy Trinity.

★

From the facts that have been adduced from spiritual science it follows that the transition that the individual human being makes from working on his lower bodies on the soul level to working on them on the spiritual level—in other words, the transition from the spiritualised consciousness soul to the Spirit-Self—will be a particularly important moment in the evolution of humanity. According to spiritual science, the mission of the Russian people, and in a wider sense the whole of the Slavic world, is connected with the fulfilment of this central task of future earthly evolution.[5] From this it becomes understandable why spiritual science speaks of the Russian people as the 'Christ people'.[6] For the intention is that the first step on the path from the consciousness soul to the Spirit-Self will be accomplished by that same people that is to lay the foundation for the whole subsequent process of the 'enchristening' of humanity. On the social plane this will lead to the realisation on Earth of a true togetherness in spirit,★ a new social community of human beings based on their brotherly union, on their permeation

---

★ Translator's note: The author here uses a virtually untranslatable Russian word 'sobornost' deriving from 'sobor' (cathedral; council). 'Cathedralhood' would be the nearest English equivalent.

8

by a common Spirit of Love (thus in the Book of Revelation such a community is called 'Philadelphia').

It is true that this work on the three lower bodies at the highest spiritual level, that is, the principal mission of the Russian people, belongs to a far distant future. What will then be possible to accomplish amongst the widest circles of mankind can in our time be attained only by individuals on the path of modern Christian initiation presented in Anthroposophy. In order to understand what this is, the following needs to be taken into consideration.

As has already been said, the highest stage of ego development within the framework of the three soul members is its full awakening in the consciousness soul. To this stage corresponds the *objective knowledge* that is directed towards the outer world, the strictest and most objective form of which is modern science, in many respects the determining characteristic of our epoch; whereas even the first steps on the path to the *spiritual* transformation of the three lower bodies will be connected with the awakening within man of higher, supersensible faculties, which also unfold in three successive stages. In anthroposophical literature they are referred to as the stages of Imagination, Inspiration and Intuition.[7] They correspond in man to the conscious awakening of the individual ego in the Spirit-Self, the Life-Spirit and Spirit-man, and lead him directly into the spiritual world.

From a spiritual-scientific point of view, the supersensible world 'behind' the physical consists essentially of actual spiritual beings. The three categories of such beings which have the most direct relationship to man and his evolution are in Christian tradition called the Angels, Archangels and Archai. Of these, the Angels, who stand in their development immediately 'above' man, basically fulfil the role of guiding individual human beings. Hence they are called 'Guardian Angels'. The Archangels fulfil a different task as spiritual beings. Their task consists in guiding individual peoples. What is usually defined by the abstract concept of 'Folk Spirit' is for modern spiritual science an actual supersensible being belonging to the Hierarchy of the Archangels.

The Russian people, too, has such a 'Folk Spirit' or 'Folk Archangel'. Thus a knowledge of his existence and of the tasks with which he has been entrusted in the general evolution of humanity is necessary not only for a real understanding of our bylina but also for Russian history as a whole.

Finally, what is usually abstractly designated as a 'Time Spirit' or the 'Spirit of an age' is also for spiritual science an actual supersensible being, who in the series of the ascending Hierarchies stands one level higher than the Archangels and belongs to the Hierarchy of the Archai, or Primal Beginnings. In contrast to a 'Folk Spirit', however, who guides the people entrusted to him throughout its earthly existence, the 'Time Spirits' alternate successively from one epoch to another.[8]

In our time, according to spiritual science, the task of the ruling Time Spirit is entrusted to that high spiritual being who in Christian tradition is known under the name of the Archangel Michael.[9] Although belonging originally to the Hierarchy of the Archangels, he has in our present epoch risen a stage higher and, as the new Time Spirit, is at the forefront of the whole evolution of humanity.*

These three categories of spiritual beings, together with those standing at a still higher level, are discerned by the modern initiate when he consciously enters the spiritual world and passes through three successive stages.

Thus the first stage of supersensible knowledge, that of *Imagination*, endows him with the capacity of beholding in full consciousness the outward revelations (manifestations) of the various spiritual beings of the higher worlds *in images*. At the second stage, that of *Inspirative* knowledge, the possibility opens up before him not only of beholding but also of spiritually listening to the deeds of spiritual beings, which are to him like the majestically sounding harmony of the spheres. This is a higher stage of penetration into the supersensible world. Finally, at the highest stage, *Intuition*, the modern initiate acquires the capacity not only of 'outwardly' beholding the images of spiritual beings and perceiving (listening to) their deeds but of experiencing their *inner essence* through completely merging with them, though without the loss of his individual ego-consciousness.[10]

---

* From a spiritual-scientific point of view, Michael may be called the 'Countenance of Christ', the bearer of the new Christ Revelation for our time.

The focal point of the path of initiation presented in Anthroposophy is the supersensible experience of the living Christ as the Son of God and as the sublime Ruler of *all* the heavenly Hierarchies. On this path Christ is first perceived in Imagination as an image, as a supersensible manifestation; then in Inspiration, when through the apprehending of His Creative Word there is revealed to the initiate the essence and full significance of His deeds both in the cosmos and also on the Earth; and finally, the initiation culminates in a *real* merging with Christ in Intuition, which leads to a direct experience of His constant presence and ceaseless activity in the ego, man's holy of holies. This is that stage of inner development at which the words of Paul the Apostle, 'It is no longer I who live, but Christ who lives in me' (Galatians 2: 20), become the highest and most central experience of the Christian initiate.[11]

It was from such a higher experience of Christ, as attained by the modern Christian initiate, Rudolf Steiner, that the Anthroposophy or spiritual science founded by him flowed.[12]

Having attained these three stages of higher knowledge to a high degree, Rudolf Steiner was in a position to carry out spiritual research in the supersensible worlds, the results of which he then set forth in his lectures (over six thousand in all) and books.[13]

However, the results of this supersensible research comprise knowledge not only of the 'good' beings of the spiritual world but also the 'evil' beings who oppose them. For apart from the Angels, Archangels and Archai who serve the divine world order, that is, who directly serve the Christ, in each of the three categories there are also beings who gradually lagged behind their brothers and then, at a certain moment in world evolution, broke away from them, since which time they have represented in the world order not the divine will but *their own*. Thus they can also be designated as servants of evil or representatives of Antichrist, in opposition to those rightly evolved hierarchic beings who serve the Christ.

Spiritual science distinguishes three categories of such fallen beings and refers to them in accordance with the names of their 'leaders'—Lucifer, Ahriman and Asura. From the hierarchic point of view one can say that the Luciferic beings are Angels who have fallen from the divine path of evolution; the Ahrimanic beings are

11

fallen Archangels; and the Asuras are fallen Archai.[14] Moreover, the higher that these fallen beings stood originally, the more powerfully the impulse of evil is now manifested through them and the more fully the essential nature of the anti-Christian forces—that is, of Antichrist himself—is expressed within them.

As has been already observed, the entire cultural-historical evolution of humanity is concerned with the gradual working of the individual ego through the three soul members, as a result of which it becomes increasingly self-aware. The opposing powers are also involved in this process. The Luciferic beings are the first to approach man—when he begins to experience his independent ego in the sentient soul, and from here they extend their influence over the other two soul members. These beings in particular tempt man with all forms of pride, self-importance, overestimation of himself, and also incline him towards lower passions and desires. Ahrimanic beings, on the other hand, approach man especially when his ego awakens in the intellectual soul or soul of character. There they strive to awaken all conceivable varieties of fear, and also bring an inclination towards lies of every kind and, above all, towards the principal lie of our time, which is manifested in materialism and in its most radical exemplification, Bolshevist ideology. Finally, the Asuras approach man when his ego is fully revealed in the consciousness soul. This time in the evolution of humanity corresponds approximately to our present epoch and to the immediate future.[15]

According to Rudolf Steiner, the first symptoms of the Asuras' activity can be discerned in the night life of the big cities, where their influence is manifested in 'wild orgies of meaningless sensuality'. In these 'orgies' are exuded the 'grotesque poisons of fire of those spirits whom we call the Asuras'. And as the fullest revelation of the individual ego dawns in the consciousness soul, it is against this that the efforts of these beings are primarily directed. Hence Rudolf Steiner also characterises them as the spirits who gradually destroy man's ego, thereby bringing about the sickness and death of all earthly culture.[16]

This last indication of the modern Christian initiate is of particular relevance to the present situation in Russia, where the symptoms of the pernicious, ego-destroying influence of this third and most powerful category of demonic forces, which, alongside all the positive possibilities for development, have begun to filter in as a replacement for Bolshevism, are appearing with ever increasing intensity.

From a spiritual-scientific point of view, all three categories of opposing forces can also be characterised in the following way. The Luciferic powers endeavour to chain humanity to the past, to stages of its development through which it has already passed. They want to send man back to a condition of cosmic childhood, where he will, it is true, be able to preserve a fairly high level of spirituality, but this spirituality will be founded solely upon a dim consciousness that is bereft of the light of reason. In contrast, Ahriman strives to tempt man with a high, though inwardly utterly cold, numbing intellectualism. He entices him in a distorted way with a future whose forces are premature and exert a paralysing influence upon souls that are not yet ready for them. As a result of this, everything of a spiritual nature is presented to such souls as merely a by-product of the material world, and the totalitarian state becomes a social 'ideal'. Finally, the Asuras seek to destroy the ego itself as the focus and promise of man's individual immortality, that is, to sever him from the sphere of the eternal in which his true being has its origin.[17]

Only a turning towards Christ—who works in our time through the mediation of the Time Spirit, Michael, who serves Him—can help men to withstand the forces of the threefold temptation in his soul. An inner sense of the constant presence of Christ overcomes the temptation of Lucifer in the soul. A living experience of the deeds of Christ and above all the highest of them, His victory over death on the Hill of Golgotha, protects against the allures of Ahriman. And a complete union of the individual ego with Christ, in the sense of the words of Paul the Apostle cited above, prevents man from succumbing to the Asuras.

Anthroposophy, the path to this threefold experience of Christ, came into being at the time when the world was about to undergo severe trials. It is these imminent events, in as far as they were to influence the history of Russia, which the prophetic bylina relates.

The Spiritual Content of the Bylina

The prophetic bylina *How the Holy Mountains Released the Mighty Russian Heroes from their Rocky Caves* originated in the 1920s in the north of Russia, in one of the villages of the Vologda region. In 1925 Professor N. Misheyev wrote it down, and in 1938 it was for the first time published by him abroad.

Misheyev describes the peasant woman, from whom he first heard and in whose words he wrote down the new bylina, as a true seeress. In his words, during the narration of the bylina she was in so real a way beholding something 'behind' those present that he even wanted to 'glance round' to see the invisible object for himself. This initial experience of Misheyev is fully confirmed by the spiritual content of the bylina, which will be spoken of below. Then Misheyev reports: 'The old woman to whom I was listening was over 80 years of age, though she was remarkably hale and hearty, and had an ardent, albeit somewhat severe look. She was known as Granny Pelageya, and it was evident that she wielded considerable authority.'[18] All the people regarded her with a profound respect, even to the extent that the old story-teller had no fear of entering into argument with the Red commissars—the representatives of the Bolshevik authorities—when they came to the village. 'When the various commissars come to us she steps on their tails, and her tongue is sharper than a knife,' reported one of the peasants to Misheyev.

There is no doubt that these face to face meetings of the visionary story-teller with the representatives of the 'new authority' brought about the direct spiritual perception of the demonic being of Bolshevism, together with its supersensible inspirer, which was to find expression in the bylina. Thus the bylina can give the reader invaluable help not only in understanding the way in which

14

supersensible forces and beings have actually participated in Russian history but also in gaining a deeper understanding of its principal feature in the 20th century—Bolshevism.

★

The narrative of the bylina begins with a short, though highly important, introduction, where reference is made to the principal stages of the natural initiation of the story-teller herself. This initiation consists of three stages, which she defines as the intellect, the prophetic (visionary) reason and the listening heart which hearkens to 'godly conversation'. In these it is not difficult to sense an echo of inner experiences which correspond to the stages of outward, objective knowledge, Imagination and Inspiration on the modern path of initiation. Subsequently, these three stages appear again and again in various situations of the bylina story, where they refer to the path leading from intellectual thinking to clairvoyant contemplation (visionary reason), and from this to listening with the heart, to an inspirative perception of the events and secrets of the future.

The first part of the bylina begins with a description of the conduct of the Russian heroes after their victory over the Mongols, who represent an outward manifestation of the Luciferic impulse in Russian history.[19] Having withstood the pressure of the Luciferic forces from without, the heroes immediately afterwards succumb to their influence from within, in their own souls. According to the bylina, once they have given up their clairvoyant 'reason' they place their hopes entirely on their earthly 'intellect' and, employing only head wisdom, immediately become immeasurably conceited and boast that they could even do battle with the heavenly powers themselves. The consequence of this swaggering is that *two heavenly warriors* appear before them, and as a result of their battle with them the heroes are forced to flee and, taking refuge with Svyatogor, become prisoners of the holy mountains.

Of the five Russian heroes mentioned in the bylina, three are of particular significance: Ilya, Dobrynya and Alyosha (the significance of the other two will be considered later). In the entire cycle of Russian bylini they occupy the central place and personify the

15

three soul members of man's being characterised in the previous section: his sentient soul (Ilya), intellectual soul or soul of character (Dobrynya) and consciousness soul (Alyosha). As has been shown, the temptation of Lucifer stems initially from the realm of the sentient soul. However, because of the still immature state of the consciousness soul of the Russians the succumbing to temptation in this case begins with this member. It starts with Alyosha, who at the beginning of the bylina appears as the bearer of just such an immature—and hence easily swayed towards materialism—consciousness soul. Thus he it is who entices the other heroes towards taking pride in their purely outward earthly strength, towards boasting in the wisdom of their heads alone. Once it has arisen in the consciousness soul, this Luciferic temptation quickly spreads to the two other members of Russian man, as represented by the figures of Dobrynya and Ilya.

Thus the Luciferic temptation is directed here against earthly evolution as a whole. It tries to turn it back and lead it in a reverse, descending direction of evolution, from the consciousness soul to the intellectual soul, or soul of character, and from it to the sentient soul, where the influence of Lucifer is at its strongest. If this were to happen, Lucifer would succeed in ensnaring Russian man in his net for ever. In the bylina this reversed movement of evolution, which has the aim of alluring man with the turn towards a more ancient, atavistic state of being, thus depriving him of all possibility of finding the true path into the future, is represented in the form of the battle of the heroes with the 'heavenly warriors', who personify the forces and impulses of a right evolution and against whom advances first Alyosha, 'the first to have boasted' (I, 8), then Dobrynya and finally, Ilya.

This sequence is completely at variance with the classical order in the individual tales about them in the whole cycle of Russian bylini. Here the accounts of their exploits are arranged 'by seniority', in accordance with the heroes' age, i.e. in the direction of the general course of evolution and not against it. First there is a cycle of bylini about Ilya, then about Dobrynya and only then about Alyosha.

As punishment for their pride, the Russian heroes henceforth remain in their rocky prison, and 'in the darkness' are unable to perceive anything with their outward, physical senses and with the intellect that is connected with them; they now again turn towards the higher forces of their souls, towards the hearing, seeing and all-comprehending 'reason'. And what is now revealed to them is the enslaving of the whole of Holy Russia by 'Krivda' that has taken place in their absence:

> How Krivda went roving through Holy Russia,
> Krivda, the heathen, the infidel,
> How she devours the orthodox people,
> Shuts the churches of God
> And murders the men of Russia.   (II, 8–12)

'Krivda', which in Russian is the opposite of 'truth', is in the bylina a being that consists wholly of falsehood. And falsehood in our cosmos is engendered by Ahriman. Hence the 'Krivda' in the bylina may be thought of as the mighty Ahrimanic being standing behind Bolshevism. Especially the sections in the bylina which relate how Krivda 'shuts the churches of God' and 'murders the men of Russia' correspond precisely to the very first measures of the Bolsheviks with regard to religion and the beginning of the Red Terror. One small detail testifies to the fact that the figure of Krivda, together with her hosts, represents the Bolshevik invasion: in part IV the narrator characterises the 'army of Krivda' as a *red beast* (IV, 83–4).

In the lecture which he gave in Stuttgart on 13 June 1920[20] Rudolf Steiner also refers to this 'bestial' nature of Bolshevism, saying that in it '... the intellectuality of the human beast, of human animality, is working its way to the surface of human evolution'. According to him, in Bolshevism 'the beast wants to emerge as the most highly intelligent animal. And he wants to transform all ... those Ahrimanic forces which have the aim of excluding [from earthly evolution] everything of a specifically human nature into impulses which can mould humanity.'

The thirteenth chapter of the Book of Revelation tells of the future manifestation of the beast. Here we also find a reference to red as the colour of the dragon that fights against 'the Woman clothed with the Sun', who represents the heavenly Sophia

17

(Revelation ch. 12). It is further said of this dragon that it was he who 'gave authority to the beast' (13: 2). Of course, the images of the Apocalypse are primarily concerned with a far more distant future. However, the future trials which they depict, trials which will eventually fall to the lot of the whole of humanity, may be heralded already in our time as a portent of the future, and it is essential that they are rightly understood by human beings.

If we return to the content of the bylina, we may now sense even more clearly the breath of the hellish abyss which is concealed behind the figure of Krivda and from which the latter derives her power. Thus as they sit in the rocky caves, the Russian heroes hear with their spiritual ears the words of the Antichrist himself from the lips of Krivda:

'I, Krivda, am stronger than all else in the world,
I am a match for any host,
Even Christ Himself,
              the Lord of Heaven!'   (II, 13–15).

When they see and hear this, the Russian heroes suffer 'great torment, a torment of hell and torture' (II, 3–4), in that they do not have the strength to be of help in this unspeakable misery, to free the soil of Russia from Krivda, to save its Christian folk from her grasp. However, their suffering gradually strengthens their spiritual vision (especially in their leader, Ilya), which now penetrates from the head to the heart and awakens within it the faculty of perceiving spiritual Inspirations:

A great cry came straight from his heart   (II, 22).

And then what thus arose in Ilya's heart as a higher inspirative faculty now ascends into the realm of the head:

And from his heart it passed to
              his grey-haired head   (II, 23)

What Ilya now experiences forms the content of a deep Christian mystery of which anthroposophical spiritual research speaks. This mystery is as follows. In the life-body of each person who is incarnated on Earth there is a supersensible stream of spiritual substance which is constantly ascending from the heart to the head and then beyond, thus uniting man with the spiritual world that surrounds him. In the course of higher development the emanations of this stream can be clairvoyantly perceived as a kind of aura around the head, or as a radiant halo similar to those depicted in icons. Since the time of the death on Golgotha and Resurrection of Christ, a significant change can be discerned in this supersensible stream. For as a result of Christ's union with the whole of earthly evolution the real presence and activity of the power of Christ can be found in the spiritual substance referred to, and this enables anyone who has attained to this experience to enter with full consciousness into the spiritual world.[22] Supported by this power of Christ, he is then enabled to behold the spiritual cosmos and ascend with his consciousness to its highest regions. This is what now happens with Ilya. The union with the spiritual stream ascending from the heart to the head reveals to him, as he prays, the cosmic sphere of Mary-Sophia, the sphere of the divine-spiritual Hierarchies which reaches to the throne of Christ Himself.

Later in the bylina there follows a detailed description of Mary-Sophia's prayer for the Russian heroes at the throne of Christ. And this is followed by the *command* of Christ—directed to 'Michael the Archangel and Yegory the Brave' (III, 23–24)—to gather all the heavenly Hierarchies (of which six are mentioned by name) so that they might accompany Mary-Sophia 'through the seven heavens' to the Earth. After descending to the Earth she frees the heroes from their centuries-long imprisonment in the rocky caves of Svyatogor.

Anthroposophy can, again, render invaluable service in the understanding of this part of the bylina; and indications can be found in it from modern spiritual research regarding the manifold activity of the spiritual Hierarchies, which work creatively in our cosmos out of the forces of the Sophia, and also a description of the sevenfold structure of the spiritual world, of which Dante bore witness in his *Divine Comedy*. However, it is only through the science of the spirit that these profound secrets can become

19

accessible to a modern consciousness, though now not as a poetic image but as an actual spiritual reality.[23]

The appearance of Mary-Sophia in the bylina has a further, quite particular significance. In a remarkable way she is throughout the narrative repeatedly identified with 'our moist Mother Earth' (II, 24). This detail of the bylina narrative testifies to the existence amongst the Russian people of the knowledge that the Russian earth has the property of reflecting for those living on it the higher heavenly spheres, together with the spiritual forces and beings abiding therein (in this case, above all the forces of Mary-Sophia, the spiritual Hierarchies and Christ Himself), through the element of light. The concluding words from Mary-Sophia's speech to Svyatogor, '... the holy Russian earth ... my younger sister' (III, 48–49), are a direct indication of this mystery. A historical confirmation that the Russian people had a knowledge of this mystery was that the inhabitants of Novgorod called their native soil the 'earth of the Divine Sophia'. Furthermore, in the Russian language the very name of a person who lives and works on the land, *krestyánin* (peasant), which is derived from the word *khristianin* (Christian), testifies to this.

Out of the sources of modern spiritual research, Rudolf Steiner, too, speaks about this unusual relationship of Russian people to their native soil. In one of his lectures he says: 'The secret of Russian geography is that the Russian receives from the earth the light which is first channelled to the earth and then reflected back from it. Consequently, the Russian receives from the earth what streams to it from outer regions [the spiritual cosmos]. He loves his earth, but he loves it because it is for him a mirror of the heavens.'[24] Thus whenever the Russian seeks to turn his soul to the heavens, he does not raise his eyes proudly toward the mountains but looks humbly down to the earth. And if the connection with the spiritual world needs to be developed into a real, supersensible experience, he will even 'prostrate himself' to it, which, as we shall see, is what Ilya does at the decisive moment.

Purified by suffering, the Russian heroes are finally able to come forth from the bowels of the holy mountains in freedom. But they do not leave their prison of many centuries in the order contrary to earthly evolution but, instead, in the sequence that corresponds to it: first Ilya, then Dobrynya and then Alyosha, who is followed by two more heroes.

In connection with this point in the bylina, Professor Misheyev reports a further conversation between the peasants who had come to listen to the bylina and its clairvoyant narrator, in which they expressed their complete confidence that if the Russian heroes had died or been turned to stone this was only for a while and they would soon revive; and if they had only been incarcerated in the rocky caves on account of their sins, they would soon come forth in freedom and liberate the Russian earth. In this extraordinary dialogue is contained the dim knowledge living amongst the simple Russian folk of the existence of reincarnation, the idea of which is, in principle, very close to the general psychological mood of Eastern Europe.

After the heroes have been set free, they must—in the person of their leader, Ilya the peasant's son—atone for their former pride and the temporary succumbing to the Luciferic forces associated with it. Now Ilya Muromets, the bearer of the sentient soul of the Russian people, must—alone—meet and overcome in his soul Lucifer, who makes every effort to lull to sleep (IV, 29) the higher spirit-consciousness awakening in the Russian hero, to force him to forget (IV, 36) about the higher task that he has voluntarily undertaken. And only when Ilya has decisively spurned all the temptations of the unknown spiritual being who 'twines round Ilya with its sweet whispering' (IV, 28) does this being, as it withdraws, finally reveal to him its true nature as a Luciferic demon of the night and appears to the Russian hero in the form of a 'witch' and a 'snake' (IV, 46–47). In the Biblical story of the Fall (Genesis, ch. 3), Lucifer is spoken of as appearing in the form of a serpent. That all the heroes apart from Ilya are asleep is indicative of the fact that the forces of the intellectual soul, or soul of character, and the consciousness soul are as yet only feebly developed. However, in this case the heroes' falling asleep is not contrary to the path of human evolution. For the two higher soul members are to evolve only gradually. Hence the heroes do not at this point fall asleep as a result of temptation but with the permission of Ilya, who alone, as the representative of the sentient soul, remains awake for them all.

Once they have withstood this trial and been delivered from the

21

inner soul charms of Lucifer, the Russian heroes can now begin the battle with a far mightier foe—Krivda. And they advance against her not merely in the order corresponding to the right, ascending evolution of humanity but by forming around her the magic sign of a cross in a circle: Ilya in front, Dobrynya on the right, Alyosha on the left, Ivan behind, and Vasily on all sides wherever his help is needed (IV, 70–77).

There then follows an impressive description of Krivda herself, the demonic being of a highly Ahrimanic nature standing behind and inspiring Bolshevism, who is clairvoyantly perceived by the Russian story-teller.

> She appeared in all her vastness,
> Facing him with one eye, standing lopsided,
> Muzzle of hound instead of face,
> Licking herself with a tongue
> a verst long   (IV, 90–93).

For thirty days, three hours and three minutes (IV, 99) the Russian heroes battle with her. The very number 333, half the number of the beast of the Apocalypse (Revelation ch. 13), is to prepare the listener for the revelation of the mystery that behind Krivda still mightier Satanic powers are concealed. Another number is set over and against this—for Ilya is armed with a mace weighing forty poods (IV, 95). The number forty is indicative of the hero's direct connection with the spiritual world. Forty days was the time that passed between Christ's Resurrection and His Ascension. In the life of the soul after death it corresponds to that moment of its final union with the spiritual sphere.

However, every time that Ilya prepares to deliver the death stroke to Krivda with his mighty mace she suddenly disappears, as though someone who is as yet invisible to the spiritual vision of the heroes and is even mightier than she on each occasion saves her from the onslaught of the Russian heroes, and the power of Krivda and the numerical strength of her 'black host' (IV, 99) become all the greater.

Having become convinced of the impossibility of defeating Krivda with human powers alone, Ilya 'falls to the moist Mother

Earth' (IV, 107, 109), that is, he turns through the mediation of the light reflected by the Russian earth to the Mother of God (IV, 108–09), to the forces of the cosmic sphere of Mary-Sophia, with his clairvoyant reason (Imaginative consciousness). But only when he succeeds in rising to the next stage, the 'listening heart' (corresponding to Inspirative consciousness), is he able to hear the quiet, barely audible answer from the hidden depths of his soul, from the divine-spiritual powers constantly present within it:

'Twas to his heart, as he turned, that his soul
softly murmured,
That some force unearthly, not of heaven,
Not of heaven, but from the depths below,
Stands by Krivda's side,
Goading her on unwearyingly
                in the fight   (IV, 114–18).

In this answer the mystery of Krivda's connection with the 'forces from the depths' (the forces of the abyss), that is, the sphere of Antichrist, is unveiled to Ilya for the first time. Behind the Ahrimanic demon of Bolshevism there gradually begins to appear the form of its unearthly master.

Only when all *human* powers have been exhausted in the battle with evil are the Russian heroes sent help from the higher worlds. They suddenly notice another hero in their midst, whom they recognise as Yegory the Brave, one of the 'two heavenly warriors' (I, 7) against whom they had sought to pit themselves when they had fallen prey to a Luciferic pride and had 'forgotten their service to Orthodox Russia' (IV, 134). Only now, having passed through all the torments and sufferings of imprisonment in the holy mountains and made the great vow that they will

... serve in faith and in truth,
In faith and in truth, the holy land of Russia,
Our own Russian Orthodox people ...   (II, 34–36)

are the heroes worthy not only to behold the heavenly warrior but also to recognise him (IV, 128).

This high spiritual being, who in the bylina is called Yegory the

Brave and can be recognised only by one who has, with his whole heart, made a vow of sacrificial service to Holy Russia, is none other than the Folk Spirit who guides the Russian people from the higher worlds and who belongs to the Hierarchy of the Archangels. He it is whom the clairvoyant story-teller perceives through the figure of Yegory, who is simply a means of expressing her purely spiritual vision.

That it is not the legendary saint and martyr George—or indeed a human being at all—who is being spoken of here is made apparent through the fact that Christ addresses Himself in the spiritual worlds simultaneously to the Archangel Michael and Yegory the Brave (III, 23–24), and also because they appear on two occasions *together* before the Russian heroes (see I, 6–7 and VI 8–14). Michael subsequently turns to Yegory as his 'sworn brother' (VI, 24), that is, as a spiritual being belonging to the same Hierarchy of the Archangels as himself.

However, more than anything else it is his description which offers the clearest indication of Yegory's high hierarchic origin. In the bylina he is called the 'protector of the land of Holy Russia' (V, 25); he speaks with a pure angelic voice (V, 14),★ and his eyes burn with a fire—issuing from his heart—filled with 'love for the land of Holy Russia' (V, 33). Yegory the Brave is indescribably beautiful; he is permeated with light, radiates gold and silver, shimmers with pearls and is strewn with celestial stars (see V, 26–30). As we read this deeply poetic description, the impression arises that it would hardly be possible to convey a more beautiful and artistic impression of the sublime appearance of the Archangel of the Russian people.

The continual prefixing of his name with the word 'light': 'light Yegory' (V, 5, 8, 25, 31, 35, 41, etc.), is a particularly clear indication of the important mystery of the relationship of the Folk

---

★ According to Dionysius the Areopagite's teaching about the Hierarchies, the words 'Angel' and 'angelic' can be used to refer to the Hierarchy of the Angels that is nearest to man and also as a general term for all hierarchical beings of a higher rank. Thus in accordance with the second meaning of this word, an Archangel can also be called 'angelic'. (See Dionysius the Areopagite, *Of the Heavenly Hierarchy*.)

Archangel with his people. For although such a relationship has in essence a purely spiritual character, nevertheless it needs a certain mediating power, which the Archangel finds amongst earthly elements. In this connection modern spiritual research indicates that for the Russian Folk Archangel the element of light represents this outward mediating power. (For other peoples, other elements are the mediators.)[25] This fact is directly connected with the special relationship of the Russian to his earth, as described above, and with the role that the experience of light plays in this.

The spiritual perception that the Russian heroes have of 'light Yegory' is above all a source of comfort to them (V, 15), in that he forgives them (V, 18) for their former pride and then restores to them all the strength that they have expended in the battle (V, 23).

In passing through these difficult trials, the heroes have been raised to a new, higher stage of inner development where the voice of the consciousness soul, matured and purified in suffering, can be heard. Its representative, the youngest of them, 'young Alyosha, who was the first to boast in times of old' (V, 34), is now the first to ask 'light Yegory' the decisive question about the reasons why the heroes had not recognised him when they met him 'on the Safat River' and had, in their blindness, even entered into battle against him. In answer to this Yegory tells Alyosha and the other heroes about the baneful influence of pride and an immoderate enthusiasm for the outward achievements of earthly civilisation (external power) upon man's higher faculties, upon his visionary reason, upon his heart that listens to the words of the spirit (V, 46–49) and which then cannot hear supersensible inspirations and loses its connection with the Folk Archangel.

This dialogue—the only prolonged one in the bylina—which in response to Alyosha's question Yegory conducts with the heroes: 'firstly for you is my teaching, but good advice for all' (V, 43), testifies to the particular significance which the Russian Archangel attaches to the right development of the consciousness soul amongst the Russian people. The reason for this is that in future it will be upon the Russian people that the task will be placed of making the transition from the highest soul member to the spiritual realm, in other words, from the consciousness soul to the Spirit-Self (see ch. 1). The foundation for the right development of the consciousness soul has already been laid by the *question* of Alyosha, which is essentially a Russian metamorphosis of the Parsifal question and is at the same time a first approach on the part of the heroes to the central spiritual stream of earthly evolution, which goes back to the Mystery of Golgotha. Rudolf Steiner says in this connection: 'For the ascending stream in human evolution has its foundation in this ability to ask questions. Since the Mystery of Golgotha there have necessarily been two streams in human evolution: one which bears the Christ-impulse in itself and gradually leads upwards to the spiritual heights; and the other which is in a sense a continuation of the descent and leads to the material life, to materialism ... In the spiritual stream we must learn to ask. Whereas in the materialistic stream everything discourages people from asking questions.'[26]

The most important quality of the consciousness soul, as distinct from the intellectual soul, or soul of character, and still more from the sentient soul, is its fundamental aspiration not merely to believe but to know. Hence with the *question* of Alyosha there arises for the first time in the bylina the problem of supersensible *knowledge*; and this knowledge must be nourished not with pride and self-importance but with true modesty and reverent respect.

This highly important soul quality is also the cornerstone of the modern path of initiation.[27]

> 'Boastful words, hasty and loud,
> Darken the understanding which the Lord God has
> given'   (V, 46–47)

says Yegory to the heroes, and continues:

> 'And without the radiance of reason, 'tis dark night
> in the heart'   (V, 48).

These words, spoken in answer to the youngest of the heroes, may with justice be regarded as a guiding-star on the path towards man's new, and wholly conscious, entry into the higher worlds.

The teaching of the Folk Archangel has a considerable spiritual influence upon the Russian heroes, and as a result they are in a position significantly to strengthen in themselves the influence of the Christ-permeated spiritual stream that flows from the heart to the head.

> And light Yegory's words of goodness
> Went right to the heroes' ardent hearts   (VI, 1–2).

And then quite concretely:

> They laid [it] in their hearts, let [it] shine forth
> in their minds   (VI, 3).

Only now, having gained conscious access to the stream of spiritual substance that lives within them, are the Russian heroes able to 'recognise' the *second* 'heavenly warrior' with whom they, in their blindness, tried to battle on the Safat River (see the first part of the bylina). This is light Yegory's sublime companion—the Archangel Michael.

One can only be amazed at how exactly and concretely the relationship between the heroes' awareness of the spiritual stream flowing from the heart to the head and their supersensible 'recognition' of the Sun Archangel is shown in the bylina:

> And no sooner had they laid this in their hearts

(What is meant here is Yegory's teaching, which furthers the spiritualisation of the consciousness soul.)

> Laid it in their hearts,
>   let it shine forth in their minds,
> Than they saw by the side of Yegory the Brave
> Another warrior, bright, ever so bright,
>   great and mighty ...
> And when they knew him,
>   all as one man dropped on their knees ...
> They bowed down before the Archangel Michael,
>   Arch-General of the heavenly powers
>   (VI, 6–9, 11–14).

27

From this it is evident that not pride but *modesty*, a modesty *accompanied by true knowledge*, opens to the Russian people the path towards the service of all mankind, towards the service not only of their Folk Archangel but of the 'Countenance of Christ', the Time Spirit Michael, the ruling spirit of all humanity. In contrast, all boasting, all arrogant appropriation for oneself of special missions and singular tasks (as has happened more than once over the course of Russian history) really only leads the Russian people away not only from service to the Christian ideals common to all humanity but also from the service of the ruling spirit of their own people.

Having become aware of and overcome their former mistakes and, hence, become worthy of meeting the guiding spirit of our time, the Russian heroes prepare once more for battle. Now Michael himself summons and leads them to 'the last battle to the death with Krivda' (VI, 21). And again they advance against her in the order corresponding to the right evolution of mankind: first Ilya, second Dobrynya, third Alyosha, and behind him Ivan and Vasily.

At this point it is necessary to say a few words about the *number* of the heroes, which—together with the two supersensible helpers—forms a holy seven. Whereas from the standpoint of a spiritual psychology the three most well-known of the heroes, those appearing here as the foremost amongst them, represent the activity of the individual ego in the three soul members of Russian man, their overall number in the bylina—five and seven—expresses the essence of sevenfold man as described in the previous chapter. The five heroes are indicative of that fivefold man whose realisation will in future be the central task of the Russian people: physical body, life-body, soul-body, ego and the spirit working in the ego, or Spirit-Self. However, the development of the higher members, the Life-Spirit and the Spirit-Man, lies beyond the scope of the Russian people's own mission in earthly evolution, and this is therefore represented in the bylina not by earthly (human) but by supersensible (superhuman) beings.

A further possible interpretation of the number of the Russian heroes is as follows. The sequence 'Ilya—Dobrynya—Alyosha' is, as we have seen, associated with the path leading to the spiritualisation of the consciousness soul, whence in time a new spiritual

28

life will grow. The question that Alyosha poses to light Yegory represents its beginning. Then 'Ivan Gostiny, the merchant's son' (IV, 14), and 'Vaska Buslayev from free Novgorod' (IV, 15), the representative of the democratic popular government (*Vyetche*), join Alyosha. Thus we have the following picture:

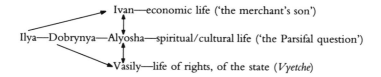

Ivan—economic life ('the merchant's son')

Ilya—Dobrynya—Alyosha—spiritual/cultural life ('the Parsifal question')

Vasily—life of rights, of the state (*Vyetche*)

The impulse of Ivan is in a sense the economic impulse of Ilya (who is 'of peasant stock', IV, 11) metamorphosed and raised to a higher level, while that of Vasily is the metamorphosis of the impulse of Dobrynya, 'the boyar's son' (IV, 12) the predecessor of the future Russian nobility and the foundation of the rights life of Tsarist Russia. Thus the bylina testifies to the Russian people's inner predisposition for the Threefold Social Order.[28]

As we return to the narrative of the bylina, we see that now, in this new battle with Krivda, the Russian heroes are battling not only against 'one-eyed Krivda' but against 'her unknown guardian' who stands behind her (VI, 37). This word 'unknown' plays a key role in the part of the bylina under consideration. For hitherto the Russian heroes and even light Yegory who guides them have not yet discerned who really stands *behind* Krivda. And so a battle is being waged not 'between man ... but between the powers of Heaven and forces from the depths' (VI, 39–42); between the Russian Folk Archangel and the Time Spirit, Michael, on the one hand, and the unknown protector of Krivda on the other.

There then follows one of the most gripping episodes of the entire bylina. For there is a highly dramatic description of how at the last moment even light Yegory himself is unable fully to avoid falling into an error from which, however, the Archangel Michael saves him by 'cutting off her [Krivda's] head with his fiery sword'. Only now is the true aspect of the Antichrist, the real inspirer of Krivda, revealed to Yegory's spiritual vision and directly afterwards to that of the Russian heroes.

29

Thus with the help of the Time Spirit, Michael, the Russian Archangel recognises the true aspect of the chief antagonist of Christ in our cosmos.

> Yegory the Brave saw and recognised Antichrist.
> [And] then Krivda's host was routed and destroyed
> (VI, 72–73).

And again we see how consistently and persistently the bylina emphasises the need for *spiritual knowledge* as the fundamental demand of the modern age of Michael.

Before we turn to the seventh and final part of the bylina, we need to dwell somewhat further upon two distinctive qualities of light Yegory, behind whom, as we have seen, the true spiritual figure of the Russian Folk Archangel lies hidden. Firstly, there is his proximity to the Time Spirit, Michael, who now leads humanity— as is indicated on several occasions in the bylina (see I, 6–6; III, 23– 24; VI, 8–14, 24, 38). The following words of Rudolf Steiner, which were addressed to the small group of Russian listeners who had come to Helsinki, the capital of modern Finland, to hear his course of lectures entitled *The Spiritual Beings in the Heavenly Bodies and in the Kingdoms of Nature*,[29] testify to this connection: 'Your Folk Soul has taken upon itself on your behalf an obligation towards humanity . . . You have only to let it speak through your thoughts, feelings and will impulses and then, if you have a sense of responsibility towards your Folk Soul, you will at the same time fulfil your duty to mankind.'[30]

If we express this thought in the images of the bylina, we may say: if Russians find the path to their Folk Archangel, to light Yegory, and are wholly permeated by his impulses, it will also become possible for them to fulfil their mission with regard to humanity, which is guided in our time by the Archangel Michael. The prophetic bylina shows the Russian people this path, which leads through inner humility and penitence firstly to a knowledge of their Folk Spirit and his tasks, and then to a knowledge, and service, of the ruling spirit of the whole of Christian humanity. For the very fact that in the supersensible worlds the Russian Folk Soul has taken upon itself an obligation towards the present spiritual ruler of mankind is an irrefutable testimony to their closeness in the supersensible worlds, a closeness which is confirmed by the bylina.

The second particular characteristic of light Yegory is his youth: 'Young and ineffably beautiful is light Yegory' (V, 31); 'the ardent, youthful heart of Yegory the Brave' (VI, 43). This reference to his youth corresponds precisely with what Rudolf Steiner says about the Russian Folk Soul in the second lecture which he gave to the Russians: 'I am speaking about your Folk Soul, which indeed exists in the spiritual world. This being has to await its task in the future, and it is full of expectation, full of hope, full of confidence. If one compares this Folk Soul with the Folk Souls of Western Europe, one has the impression, on the one hand, of youthful and aspiring forces and, on the other, of old age and senility.'[31] And elsewhere in the same lecture: 'The Russian Folk Soul—a being from the Hierarchy of the Archangels—is young and full of hope; it has its task before it. And it will be up to Russian anthroposophists to find the bridge from the individual soul to the Folk Soul, and to learn to understand what the Folk Soul wants of them.' The bylina gives an indication of this task as well, when it speaks of how after the victory over Krivda and her 'black host' (IV, 98)

> The Russian heroes, the mighty men of old,
> On all sides gathered round Yegory the Brave,
> ... they surrounded light Yegory ... (VIII, 1, 2, 4).

Now the Russian heroes turn again to the spiritual world, again they 'incline to the moist Mother Earth' (VII, 15). And as the Russian heroes pray together to Yegory the Brave and the Mother of God (VII, 17), the heavenly Mary-Sophia turns to her Son with the plea that He liberate the Russian earth from the power of Antichrist. Then at her request and intercession Christ gives the Archangel Michael the order to drive the Antichrist from the land of Russia (VII, 36–38).

This role of protection and intercession which Mary-Sophia fulfils for the Russian people throughout the bylina has—from a spiritual point of view—its foundation in the fact that with the transition from the epoch of the consciousness soul to that of the Spirit-Self new sources of *Sophian*, that is to say clairvoyant, wisdom will be unveiled to humanity. And inasmuch as this transition is to be accomplished for the whole of humanity by the Russian people (and in a wider sense the Slavic peoples), their connection from the beginning with the cosmic sphere of the Sophia is thereby explained. The fact that the majority of the churches built in Russia soon after its Christianising in 988 were dedicated to the Mother of God or the Divine Sophia may be regarded as a prophetic sign of these future developments. Thus churches dedicated to the Sophia were erected in Kiev, Novgorod, Yaroslavl, Polotsk and in other towns.

★

The bylina ends with a description of the further spiritual battle which is now waged by the Archangel Michael. However, this battle is not to be identified with Michael's battle with the dragon, as described in the twelfth chapter of the Revelation of St John (7–9). For in the Book of Revelation the theme is the ultimate, apocalyptic destiny of the *whole* of mankind, whereas the bylina is concerned only with the future destiny of the land of Russia. Thus in response to His mother's request Christ says:

> 'The time is not ripe to cut off the head of
> Antichrist;
> That day and that hour are a secret profound.
> [But] the time has come for Antichrist to
> leave the holy [land of] Russia ...'   (VII, 30–32).

However, even this 'lesser battle' with Antichrist can be waged neither by the Russian heroes nor even by light Yegory but only by Michael. For upon its outcome, in a deeper sense, depends the destiny of not only the land of Russia but the whole of humanity in the age to come.

This final part of the bylina is, therefore, concerned with the third great temptation, which will make its full force felt in Russia only in the future but is already being anticipated today. And the Russian heroes will be able to withstand it only by finding the path to their Folk Archangel.

32

[They] watched the great, unprecedented battle,
And crowded round light Yegory,
                their sworn brother.   (VII, 46–47).

In order better to understand the essential nature of this third temptation, it is necessary to recall that the first temptation, which is only briefly mentioned at the beginning of the bylina, has to do with the battle of the Russian heroes with Luciferic forces (whose outward bearers were the Mongol hordes). Then in the connection with the second temptation they battle against the Ahrimanic forces of Krivda not alone but with light Yegory, the ruling Archangel of the Russian people. Finally, in the third battle, against the future mission of 'Holy Russia', even more terrible forces of darkness well forth. These are those Satanic powers which from a spiritual-scientific point of view Rudolf Steiner calls Asuric.

A reference to this aspect of evil in our world can be found in the Book of Revelation. The divinely inspired clairvoyant speaks in chapter 16 verse 13 of the false prophet, the beast and the dragon. Nevertheless, this is not as yet the apocalyptic coming of the Antichrist, which will precede the last days of the earthly aeon, but only the manifestation in the world of his dark forces *through the mediation* of the most powerful of the evil spirits who serve him. According to the bylina, only Michael, the 'Countenance of Christ' and His emissary, is able to conquer them.

And Christ, the Lord of Heaven, commands
His Arch-General, the Archangel Michael,
To drive fierce Antichrist
            from the land of Holy Russia   (VII, 36–38).

According to spiritual science, the efforts of the Asuric powers will be directed primarily towards gradually depriving man of his holiest possession, that which alone gives him the form and likeness of the divine—his ego. In Rudolf Steiner's words, they will endeavour 'to tear away [man's] ego piece by piece'.[32] Now the physical bearer of the ego in man's organism is his warm blood.[33] Thus, to express the same thing more pictorially, we may say that the Asuras will from the outset have a vampire tendency. They can also be likened to a kind of demonic bird, which with beak and claws pecks and tears out piece by piece the spiritual substance of man's ego.

The Russian clairvoyant, the creator of the prophetic bylina, now beholds this terrible mystery of the effect of the Asuric powers upon humanity. She perceives them clairvoyantly in the form of a huge black raven:

> That black raven holds in its claws
> > the Holy [land of] Russia.
> It has covered it with its wings, tears it with its claws
> > pecks it with its beak,
> With its iron beak it pecks it,
> > and drinks its warm blood   (VII, 53–55).

Again, this picture from the bylina corresponds precisely to what Rudolf Steiner says about the Asuras: 'It is not that the whole human being will necessarily succumb to them, but the Asuras will tear pieces from a person's spirit.'[34]

The counterpart in the bylina to the 'black raven' is the 'eagle', in whose form Michael is manifested to the clairvoyant story-teller (VI, 64). In both cases the eagle and the raven have a relationship to the human ego, but only in diametrically opposite senses—as, respectively, a principle that creates and a principle that destroys the ego. Moreover, the eagle is the symbol of John, the favourite disciple of Our Lord, the Evangelist and writer of the Book of Revelation, in whose 'Apocalypse' we find the only reference to the Archangel Michael in the New Testament (ch. 12). In the Gospel written by him he speaks about the deep and age-old connection of Christ with every human ego. For since the Mystery of Golgotha Christ has sought to help every human individual in that task of transforming his being out of the forces of his ego, a task which he needs to accomplish and which is to culminate in the spiritualisation of the *whole* of man's being, that is, in his complete likeness to Christ.

However, on the path towards this high ideal, mankind still has to pass through serious trials and overcome great temptations. The prophetic bylina tells us only about that aspect of them which falls to the lot of the Russian people.

The warmth living in the human blood is the earthly reflection of cosmic warmth, or fire. The Asuras endeavour to gain mastery also over this cosmic element, in order to put it to the service of the forces of extreme evil. Thus the bylina says about the Asura:

> Its eyes are a fiery hell,
> all flaming and full of malice (VII, 51).

This cosmic fire, which serves the forces of evil, outwardly sheds only a spiritual darkness which extinguishes all light and even hides the Sun from view:

> It rose all enormous, dark with eyes of fire,
> With its blackness it covered the red Sun,
> darkened the clear sky (VII, 66–67).

In the Gospel this darkness is called 'outer darkness' (Matthew 22: 13), by which is meant its essential hostility to the innermost aspect of man's being—his ego. And at Christ's command, Michael, the heavenly warrior, now enters into battle with this objective cosmic darkness. From the Eastern—Sun—side he appears on the field of battle (VII, 57) as a representative of the heavenly light, as the emissary of the Spiritual Sun.

The last battle begins. As they behold it, the Russian heroes gain the impression that the powers of darkness are prevailing; in their hearts they begin to doubt the ultimate victory of the Christ forces. 'Can it be done?'—the words escape their lips (VII, 73). However, this doubt of theirs has its source not in objective spiritual reality but only in the imperfection of the beholders' organs of spiritual perception. For the bylina speaks only of two stages of supersensible perception: visionary reason and the listening heart, corresponding respectively to Imaginative and Inspirative knowledge. The spiritual powers which become accessible to man at these two stages are sufficient only to withstand the Luciferic and Ahrimanic spirits and not the Asuras. Ultimately the attainment of a third, still higher stage of spiritual knowledge is required—that of

35

Intuition, whose powers are not as yet fully possessed by the Russian heroes.

From the standpoint of modern Christian initiation, as presented in Anthroposophy, one can say that at the first two stages of spiritual knowledge the Russian heroes become able to behold Christ and also to hear the words which He speaks to Mary-Sophia and the Archangel Michael (see parts III and VII of the bylina), which in the supersensible worlds are not mere words but deeds. Nevertheless in both cases Christ is experienced by the heroes only from outside. In their spiritual contemplation He is revealed to them as though from afar, in the heavenly heights, on His high throne (III, 18). He is not as yet fully beheld by them in the holy of holies of their own being, in their ego, as is possible at the third and highest stage of spiritual knowledge—Intuition.

Light Yegory reproves the Russian heroes in this inner weakness ('little faith', VII, 76), thereby pointing towards their principal task of receiving Christ right into their individual ego, thus wholly fulfilling the words of Paul, 'It is no longer I who live, but Christ who lives in me' (Galatians 2: 20). For upon the fulfilment of these words, which must become a real inner experience, the whole future of 'Holy Russia' is founded.

*

However terrible may be the three trials described in the bylina through which the Russian people has passed, is now passing and will continue to pass, it will be through overcoming them that it will be able to master those spiritual powers which it will need for the fulfilment of its future mission in human evolution. According to the testimony of spiritual science, this mission of the Russian people will consist in the establishing amongst mankind of a kingdom of brotherly love, 'Philadelphia', and in spreading a new spiritual culture throughout the Earth.

In the last lines of the bylina, light Yegory, the guiding Spirit of the Russian people, shares with the heroes an indication of their people's future mission when he gives them 'his true and unbreakable word'

That Antichrist, the wicked raven, will not return
to Holy Russia,
That to the holy land of Russia will come great joy,
And to the Orthodox Russian people comfort and grace'
(VII, 78–80).

How the Holy Mountains Released the Mighty Russian Heroes from their Rocky Caves

(Text of the bylina)

Where intellect suffices not, consult your reason,
For it is good, calm and wise,
Ever taciturn through godly conversation,
All-knowing and strong, awake to the call of the heart,
Your protector, your advocate before God.

I

When on the Safat River* they had slaughtered the Tartar
    hosts,
The glorious Russian heroes started boasting—
Because they had forsaken their reason
And trusted only to their intellect—
5 That now it was time they fought with unearthly powers.
And a radiant unearthly power appeared before them,
Two heavenly warriors. And the heroes knew them not.
Young Alyosha, the first to have boasted, rushed forward,
And cut the two warriors in twain—
10 But now there were not two but four.
Felled by Dobrynya Nikitich's sharp sword
These four warriors rose up as eight.
After the blows of old Ilya of Murom,

---

* A river near Kiev.

38

After Vaska Buslayev had whistled and Ivan Gostiny hurled
   his lance,
15 Four and sixty warriors arose.
The heroes then threw themselves on this host,
Shoulder to shoulder they charged, as one man,
And they started hewing and cleaving that host,
But the heavenly army went on growing,
20 Waging battle against the heroes.
The heroes grew weary, took fright and retreated,
Fled to the great and holy mountains
To seek the defence of their elder brother,
Their sworn brother, Svyatogor himself,
25 Huge, ever-sleeping Svyatogor.
They awoke their brother,
Woke and entreated him;
In fear they implored him, not speaking a word,
Sending Ilya, the peasant's son
30 And their leader, on before them.
Svyatogor rubbed his eyes, those bottomless lakes,
Drew together his eyebrows, those dreaming forests,
Shook with his yawn the steady earth;
And as he stretched himself, he touched a passing cloud,
35 Staring at Ilya with wondering amazement.
He recognised Ilya, with whom he had changed crosses,
Understood with his heart the heroes' bitter entreaty.
And he took hold of the heroes and their horses,
Stuffed them into his pockets, the deepest caverns,
40 And sank back with a sigh into endless sleep.

II

And from that deep sleep,
From that heavy, leaden sleep,
A great torment fell on the heroes,
A torment of hell and torture ...
5 For they themselves are not asleep,
They cannot sleep, or see in the dark,

39

But they can hear, and grasp all with their reason:
How Krivda went roving through Holy Russia,
Krivda the heathen, the infidel,
10 How she devours the Orthodox people,
Shuts the churches of God
And murders the men of Russia.
'I, Krivda, am stronger than all else in the world,
I am a match for any host,
15 Even Christ Himself, the Lord of Heaven!'
Thus says Krivda in her boasting,
Scoffing at the Russian people—
Wherever they live on their Mother Earth,
Wherever they roam—in their orphaned state.
20 And then old Ilya, the peasant's son,
Shouted aloud in the darkness;
A great cry came straight from his heart
And from his heart it passed to his grey-haired head:
'O Mother of God, our moist Mother Earth!
25 Forgive your youngest sons,
The ancient heroes of Russia,
Who on account of their shameful boasting
Sit in dark dungeons in the rocky mountain;
Here they have sat for long thorny ages,
30 Ages full of thorns and spikes and sharpness.
Raise from his sleep your eldest son,
Svyatogor, greatest of great heroes!
Give us our liberty, our kingly freedom,
That we may serve in faith and in truth,
35 In faith and in truth, the Holy Land of Russia,
Our own Russian Orthodox people ...
O Mother of God, our moist Mother Earth!
Hear the prayers of your youngest sons,
The mighty Russian heroes.'

III

And the heart-rending cry of Ilya, the peasant's son,
Went right through the mountains,
It rose above the passing cloud,
And flew up to the golden vaults of Heaven,
5 Then it fell and nestled like a painful lump,
A lump of pain at the throne of the Mother of God.
And the Mother of God caught sight of this painful lump,
She heard this heart-rending cry,
And took to her heart the prayer of Ilya,
10 Took it to her heart and sobbed bitterly;
And to the throne of her Son, Jesus the Saviour,
Climbing the azure steps, with bowed head,
With bowed head she quietly ascended!
She entreats her beloved Child,
15 With her tears flowing like heavy rain,
Asking pardon for the Russian heroes.
And the Saviour Himself hastens to answer the Pure One,
Christ Himself speaks on His high throne:
'O Mother beloved, blessed among all women,
20 You who intercede before me for every sinner great or small,
Through you is forgiven the heroes' boasting,
The foolish boasting of the Russian heroes'.
And the Lord of Heaven gives the order
To Michael the Archangel and Yegory the Brave
25 To gather the heavenly host and powers,
And with trumpets of Seraphim and voices of Cherubim,
On the shrouds of Archangels and the wings of Angels,
To fly down with Our Lady to the land of Holy Russia.
And numberless forces of mighty powers gathered,
30 Loudly echoed the trumpets of Seraphim,
Joyful voices of Cherubim sang forth,
Wide unfolded the robes of Archangels,
Outspread were the snow-white wings of Angels,
Receiving our Heavenly Lady, the Mother of God,
35 And with a royal flight they passed through the seven
    heavens,

Bringing our Intercessor down to the land of Holy Russia.
Then speaks the Mother of God, the moist Mother Earth:
'You mountains, my steep mountains,
Lofty mountains, stony mountains, holy mountains,
40 Open up, make way, burst asunder,
Release my youngest sons,
The mighty Russian heroes!
Their sinful boasting has been pardoned,
Their boast to conquer the heavenly host.
45 Awake, my great mountains,
Out of your deep, eternal sleep.
Free the ancient Russian heroes!
The land of Holy Russia is pining for them,
Holy Russia, my younger sister.'

IV

At the cry of the Mother of God,
At the call of the moist Mother Earth,
The stony mountains creaked and murmured and groaned.
They began shaking and rocking ...
5 They opened up, they parted, they split asunder.
Then awoke the greatest of the heroes,
That hero, huge Svyatogor himself.
He opened his pockets, those dark caves,
And out of those deep caves rode forth the glorious and
mighty heroes
10 The heroes of Holy Russia, one after the other:
Ilya of Murom, of peasant stock,
Dobrynya Nikitich, the boyar's son.
Alyosha Popovich, the parson's boy,
Ivan Gostiny, the merchant's son,
15 Vaska Buslayev from free Novgorod.
They rode forth, doffed their helmets and crossed themselves,
On all sides, on all four sides they bowed,
They tightened the girths of their goodly steeds and made
ready,

And by nightfall they had reached the Safat River.
21 Pitching their white tent by the river, they prayed,
And when they had prayed they went to sleep,
Went to sleep all except their leader,
That old Cossack, light Ilya of Murom,
The peasant's son, bearer of pain for all.
25 The heroes' sleep is deeper than the ocean,
Their snoring can be heard a hundred versts away.
'Tis not the viper but the dark night
That twines round Ilya with its sweet whispering.
'Go to sleep, Ilya, lay thee down—sleep is dearer than a
mother's breast.
30 How without sleep can you wage battle and win victory?'
Ilya listens, thinks his own thoughts and chuckles.
He twirls his grey moustache and smiles.
'Night, O, night, you stony prison!
Did Ilya sit behind your bars,
35 Listen to your songs, your calumny,
In order that old Ilya should go to sleep and forget all? ...
Ilya the peasant's son has neither slept nor dozed,
And through your songs he has heard the groan of Russia,
He has listened and cried out ... and his cry was heard.
40 Ilya has become the guardian of the peace of his
Mother Earth.
Night, O night, you stony prison!
Sweet are your songs, they entice one to sleep.
But if old Ilya falls asleep, then the end will come
To Orthodox Russia and all her children.'
45 And dark night took revenge with a fierce, cold wind.
The witch poured rain on Ilya from a suspended cloud.
The serpent prepared for a long journey ...
And on God's side, in the East, red flowers could be seen,
The bright dawn arose, playfully smiling on Ilya,
50 And blushed before the bright Sun, before the brave hero.
Ilya straightened himself up to his full hero's height,
He breathed out with a full breast.
He washed in the river, bowed to Christ,
Bent down to his Mother Earth.

55 He stood up 'What is that noise? Do I hear aright?'
He looked round—and he sees that towards the Safat
    River
There creeps a dark black cloud, threatening, ever so great.
It is the host of Krivda herself, the infidel host.
And old Ilya cries with a resounding voice:
60 'Ho, where are you, my captains, my sworn brothers?
Wake up, rise up, mount your swift steeds!
Ride to your leader, Ilya, the peasant's son.'
And the mighty heroes awoke,
The captains arose at the hero's call,
65 Prayed to Christ, mounted their good steeds
And gathered around their leader.
And Ilya Ivanovich, the peasant's son, spoke forth:
'Ho there and hail, my brave captains,
Mighty Russian heroes!
70 The old Cossack, Ilya of Murom, will approach Krivda from
    the front.
You, Dobrynya Nikitich, strike Krivda from the right!
You, Alyosha, break her cursed power from the left!
Press her hard from the rear, Ivan Gostiny!
And you, Vaska from Novgorod,
75 Strike Krivda wherever you see
That your free force is needed,
Roving and unrestrained!
Ay, strike with your youthful whooping and whistling,
That Krivda may take fright,
80 Take fright not so much of your steely sword
As your lusty whooping and whistling,
Lusty, free and unbound.'
'Twas not bright falcons swooping on the red beast
But the Russian heroes attacking the host of Krivda.
85 They began to hew and slaughter the army of Krivda.
Not only do the heroes hew
But the good steeds trample it down.
When Ilya's steel blade swings, a gap is seen!
Ilya of Murom advanced from the front towards Krivda.
90 She appeared in all her vastness,

44

Facing him with one eye, standing lopsided,
Muzzle of hound instead of face,
Licking herself with her tongue a verst* long
Ilya's forty pood* mace went swinging.
95 His eyes grew dizzy, his foot stumbled—
Fighting an empty space was beyond his power ...
When he stood up, Krivda was not there ... Yet everywhere
    in the gaps
The black army was fully there again ...
For thirty days, three hours and three minutes
100 The heroes waged their deadly battle.
Their sturdy shoulders sagged,
Their goodly steeds gave way,
Their swords of steel were blunted,
And Krivda still fought on,
105 Always bringing fresh troops into the battle.
And there he fell, Ilya the peasant's son,
He fell down to the moist Mother Earth.
'O Mother of God,
My Mother of God, moist Mother Earth!
110 Hearken now to Ilya, your son,
Your faithful, peasant son.
Not to his eyes was it given to see,
Nor to his ears was it given to hear,
'Twas to his heart, as he turned, that his soul softly
    murmured,
115 That some force unearthly, not of Heaven,
Not of Heaven but from the depths below,
Stands by Krivda's side,
Goading her on unwearyingly in the fight.'
Old Ilya rose from the earth to his feet,
120 He crossed himself as the sacred custom is;
He called his captains, his comrades,
To a last, fateful council.
They ran up, all four of them, and stood around him:
Tired, exhausted, blackened and darkened.

---

* The literal equivalent of a verst is 3500 feet, and of a pood 36 lb (16.38 kg).

125 Once Ilya had spoken, and sighed,
He noticed there were more heroes—five in all!
Marvel of marvels, wonder of wonders!
He wanted to ask, but as he looked he beheld
One of the warriors from whom he had fled to the strong mountains.
130 All the heroes identified him, and recognised
Their faithful brother, Yegory the Brave.
They bowed their heads with burning shame.
To whom they had boasted, whom had they fought, from whom had they fled?
Having forgotten their service to Orthodox Russia,
135 Where had these brave heroes hidden?
To whom abandoned the land of Holy Russia?

V

'Twas not the gentle morning breeze
Wafting over the strong and lofty oaks,
Wafting, rousing and raising their tops
After their battering by the dark night,
5 'Twas light Yegory the Brave who approached,
Approached and raised the heads of the Russian heroes,
Raised, embraced and kissed them,
Light Yegory kissed them with a smile.
It was not the lark, God's bird, in the sky,
10 Trilling its clear, morning song,
Ever warm with the Sun, to greet
The peasant's day of work and toil,
It was St Yegory with his voice,
His clear, angelic song,
15 Laughing and gently comforting the Russian worker-heroes:
'My brothers, look not at him who speaks of the past!'
With that kiss of Yegory their brother,
With his warm and cheering words of pardon,
The heroes rose to their full gigantic height,

20 They spread and straightened their mighty shoulders,
They raised their invincible heads with their iron helms,
With their right hands they gripped their steel blades,
And through their veins poured their ancient Russian
strength,
Gazing, endlessly gazing, at Yegory the Brave,
25 At light Yegory, protector of the land of Holy Russia.
Yegory's legs to the knee were of pure silver made,
His arms to the elbow were of red gold,   ? St George
His head a shimmer of pearl,
His hair of bright chestnut and all in curls,
30 Over his body myriad stars were strewn.
Young and ineffably beautiful is light Yegory,
And his eyes burn with fire from his ardent heart,
From his ardent heart, from his love for the land of Holy
Russia.
And young Alyosha, who was the first to boast in times of
old, spoke thus:
35 'Tell us, light Yegory, our benefactor,
How did we fail to recognise you then on Safat River,
Strewn as you are with myriad stars . . .?
How did we not notice you in your pure silver and red gold,
In your ineffable beauty and with your Angel's voice?
40 Had we known you, we would never have struggled and
fought.'
And light Yegory answers with his Angel's voice:
'My sworn brother, young Alyosha, mighty Russian hero,
Firstly for you is my teaching, but good advice for all:
The boastful word is ruin,
45 Self-praise is man's undoing;
Boastful words, hasty and loud,
Darken the understanding which the Lord has given,
And without the radiance of reason, 'tis dark night in the
heart . . .
Can one see or make things out, Alyosha, in the dark autumn
night?

VI

And light Yegory's words of goodness,
Went right to the heroes' ardent hearts.
They laid it in their hearts, let it shine forth in their minds,
That in all the long, eternal ages
5 None should boast or avaunt his self-importance . . .
And no sooner had they laid it in their hearts,
Laid it in their hearts and let it shine forth in their minds,
Than they saw by the side of Yegory the Brave
Another warrior, bright, ever so bright, great and mighty,
10 And when they saw him, they knew that they had fought
        him too on the Safat River.
And when they knew him, all as one man dropped on their
        knees,
All dropped on their knees, to the moist Mother Earth they
        bowed down.
The Russian heroes, confessing their sin,
Bowed down before the Archangel Michael, Arch-General
        of the heavenly powers.
15 And Archangel Michael, God's Arch-General, speaks thus:
'Bow not before me, God's servant and your servant!
Incline rather to the Lord God, Jesus Christ,
To His pure Mother, the Mother of God, your
        Intercessor! . . .
Bow down and arise, stand up, you warriors, heroes of old!
20 Sit on your good and trusty steeds.
Begin the last battle, the deathly battle with Krivda,
The deathly battle with Krivda for the defence of the land of
        Holy Russia
Encircle the pagan host of Krivda on three sides,
While the fourth, from the front, I shall take with my sworn
        brother, Yegory!'
25 The heroes arose, laden with new-gained strength;
Heavily had they leant on the moist Mother Earth;
They mounted their swift steeds, newly fortified.
With one leap their swift steeds covered a hundred versts,
Surrounding Krivda's host on three sides,

30 While the fourth they left to Archangel Michael and Yegory.
    Like the roar of wild bears flies Ilya of Murom's forty pood
        mace,
    Like an axe on the trees cuts Dobrynya Nikitich's steely
        blade,
    Like a scythe in the grass rings and hews Alyosha Popovich's
        sharp sabre,
    Hums in its flight the long lance of Ivan Gostiny,
35 And everywhere is heard the whistle and whoop of Vaska
        Buslayev.
    The Archangel Michael and Yegory the Brave
    Approach from the front the high tent of Krivda,
    One-eyed Krivda and her guardian unknown.
    Now they see a small space, not great but clear,
40 Not great but clear, between the unearthly forces,
    The heavenly powers and the powers from the depths,
    Opening up for the great battle belonging not to the world of
        men.
    And the ardent, youthful heart of Yegory the Brave was
        aflame,
    And like a bright falcon he hurled himself in front of
        Archangel Michael
45 Upon one-eyed Krivda, who watched him laughingly.
    Watched him mockingly and invitingly.
    Yegory the Brave, already close to the figure of Krivda,
    Was raising his sharp-edged lance with his left hand,
    And with his right was swinging his steely blade,
50 Was swinging it to cut off one-eyed Krivda's head,
    When ... Yegory's silver legs began to tremble,
    His golden arms grew numb,
    St Yegory's heart began to freeze,
    And he fell dumb as if crushed by a hammer;
55 His beautiful eyes were clouded,
    His ears were shrouded beneath his bright chestnut curls,
    Yegory became like a dead stone, as though fettered in
        iron ...
    Yegory had seen by Krivda's side
    Christ Himself, the Lord of Heaven,

60 Gazing at him with darkened eyes,
    Gazing in anger at Yegory the Brave ...
    'Twas no stormy whirlwind rushing from the ocean,
    Nor thunder and lightning splitting in pieces the mighty oak:
    'Twas the Archangel Michael soaring like an eagle over
        Krivda,
65 Cutting off her head with his sword of fire.
    Returning to his senses, Yegory the Brave then noticed
    That he whom he had taken to be Christ
    Gradually began to change:
    Became terrible, wild and fierce as a roaring lion,
70 Loathsome, base and cunning like a viper,
    Foul, insolent and lascivious as something evil from the
        marsh:
    Yegory the Brave saw and recognised Antichrist.
    Then Krivda's heathen host was routed and destroyed.

VII

    The Russian heroes, the mighty men of old,
    From all sides gathered round Yegory the Brave,
    From three sides to the fourth they came,
    To the fourth they came and surrounded light Yegory,
5   And at Antichrist, fierce, cunning and insolent,
    That unearthly, subterranean power, they looked in horror.
    'My brothers, mighty Russian heroes,
    Our strength is not equal to Antichrist, great, black and
        terrible!'
    So said Yegory the Brave in a low whisper.
10 'We cannot master him in battle;
    We can pray, we can turn to Christ Jesus.
    May His will be done, as in Heaven so on Earth.'
    Following Yegory, the heroes doffed their helmets, crossed
        themselves,
    With the Orthodox cross they crossed themselves, fell on
        their knees,
15 They knelt down, prayed, inclined to the moist Mother
        Earth,

For the deliverance of the land of Holy Russia from
  Antichrist.
And the prayer of the Russian heroes and of Yegory the
  Brave rose to the Mother of God,
It rose to the Virgin Mother of Christ the King of Heaven.
And the Mother of God enquires of her beloved Child:
20 'O my beloved Child, Saviour of the race of men,
Tell me, let me know, has not the time come to cut off the
  head of Antichrist,
Is not the hour at hand for him to leave the land of Holy
  Russia,
To free the Orthodox Russian people from their torments?
Is it not now the time for the Russian people to do their
  work and labour,
25 To do their work, perform their labour,
Be cleansed from their sins,
Build the churches of God and thank the Lord their God?'
And Christ, the Lord of Heaven, made answer:
'O my beloved Mother, blessed among all women,
30 The time is not ripe to cut off the head of Antichrist.
That day and that hour are a secret profound ...
The time has come for Antichrist to leave the land of Holy
  Russia,
For the Orthodox Russian people to be freed from their
  torments,
To do their work, to perform their labour, to be cleansed
  from their sins,
35 To build God's churches, and to thank the Lord their God.'
And Christ, the Lord of Heaven, commands
His Arch-General, the Archangel Michael,
To drive fierce Antichrist from the land of Holy Russia.
'My brothers, mighty Russian heroes!
40 Arise from the moist earth onto your nimble feet and stand
  upright!
Stand upright and cross yourselves, the great battle is
  beginning,
Antichrist, the fierce, the insolent, the foul, is being driven
  from Holy Russia!'

51

So speaks Yegory the Brave, looking up to Heaven and
  smiling.
The mighty heroes leapt to their nimble feet,
45 Leapt up, stood upright, crossed themselves,
And they watched the great, unprecedented battle,
And crowded round light Yegory, their sworn brother.
Fierce Antichrist, ever changing and changing, became a
  black raven,
And the length of that raven was a thousand versts, and the
  span of its wings two thousand.
50 The head of that raven is black like an enormous mountain,
Its eyes are a fiery hell, flaming and full of malice,
Its beak and claws are of iron, as sharp as can be.
It holds in its claws the holy land of Russia,
· It has covered it with its wings, tears it with its claws, pecks at
  it with its beak,
55 With its iron beak it pecks it, and drinks its warm blood.
Holy Russia groans. The black raven rejoices.
On the Eastern side, the Sun's side, the heavens have
  opened,
The heavens have opened, God's Kingdom is revealed for a
  moment,
Is revealed for a moment, and the hearts of the Russian
  heroes light up,
60 Their hearts light up, and an ineffable, eternal joy remains.
'Twas not the golden lightning, sternly flaring from God's
  Kingdom,
Nor its brother, the thunder of Heaven with its terrible stroke,
'Twas Archangel Michael, the mighty Arch-General,
At God's command, at Christ's behest going into battle with
  Antichrist.
65 Seeing the Archangel, the Antichrist raven spread its black
  wings,
It rose all enormous, dark with eyes of fire.
With its blackness it covered the red Sun, darkened the clear
  sky,
It darkened the clear sky and fell like a thousand pood stone
  upon the Archangel,

Fell like a stone, with its black wings, seemingly overwhelming him ...

70 The hearts of the Russian heroes grew cold.
They rushed to their sworn brother.
'Tell us, tell us, light Yegory,
Tell us the whole truth ... Can it be done?'
Shaking his pearly locks with a smile,

75 Yegory the Brave reproached his brothers, the Russian heroes,
Reproached them for their little faith in Christ the Saviour.
He gave them his true, unbreakable word
That Antichrist, the wicked raven, will not return to Holy Russia,
That great joy will come to the holy Russian land,

80 And to the Orthodox Russian people comfort and grace.

Translator's note:

This translation of the bylina, which is intended pre-eminently as a faithful—though also, it is hoped, readable—rendering of the Russian original, is based on the version by Gleb Struve and Bernard Pares, published by the Centenary Press, London, in 1935. I am indebted to Marianne Gorge for drawing my attention to this version. A few fine phrases have also been culled from the performing version made by the late Virginia Brett in America, kindly made available through Astrid Prokofieff by Christy Barnes—though much of it is too free for present purposes. The text has been thoroughly revised by comparing it with the Russian original and by taking into account various points made by Sergei Prokofieff in his commentary.

Author's Notes

1. St Augustine, Contra epist. Manich., 5.
2. See the list of anthroposophical literature on pp.58–60.
3. Regarding the ninefold and sevenfold structure of man's being, see Rudolf Steiner's book *Theosophy* and *Occult Science* (GA 9 and 13, Rudolf Steiner Press 1989 and 1969).
4. See Rudolf Steiner's book, *Theosophy*.
5. Regarding the mission of the Slavic peoples, see Rudolf Steiner's lectures of 30 May 1908 (morning and evening). They are the tenth and eleventh lectures in the cycle of twelve lectures given in Hamburg that were devoted to a spiritual-scientific study of St John's Gospel (GA 103, English translation published by Anthroposophic Press, New York 1962). See also the lecture of 24 June 1908, which is the seventh of twelve lectures given in Nuremberg and devoted to a spiritual-scientific study of the Book of Revelation (GA 104, English translation published by Rudolf Steiner Press, London 1977).
6. See the eighth lecture of the cycle *From Symptom to Reality in Modern History*, given in November 1918 in Dornach (nine lectures in all), English translation published by Rudolf Steiner Press, London 1976.
7. See further regarding this in the following books by Rudolf Steiner: *Knowledge of the Higher Worlds: How is it Achieved?* (GA 10, Rudolf Steiner Press 1976); *The Stages of Higher Knowledge* (GA 12, Anthroposophic Press 1974); and *Occult Science—An Outline* (GA 13, Rudolf Steiner Press 1969).
8. See Rudolf Steiner's lecture-cycle *The Mission of Individual Folk Souls in Relation to Teutonic Mythology* (the eleventh lecture, given in June 1910 in Christiania, Oslo), English translation published by Rudolf Steiner Press, 1970.
9. Regarding the mission of Michael, see Rudolf Steiner's lecture-cycle entitled *The Mission of the Archangel Michael*, six lectures given in November 1919 in Dornach (GA 194, English translation published by Anthroposophic Press, New York 1980); and also the series of articles by Rudolf Steiner under the title *The Michael Mystery*, written in 1924/1925 (GA 26, English translation, *Anthroposophical Leading Thoughts*, Rudolf Steiner Press 1969).
10. See Rudolf Steiner, *Occult Science—An Outline* (Rudolf Steiner Press 1969).
11. Ibid.

12. See Rudolf Steiner's autobiography, *The Course of My Life* (Anthroposophic Press, 1970), ch. XXVI.
13. See the Bibliographical Note on p.58.
14. See Rudolf Steiner's lecture given on 22 March 1909 in Berlin, *The Deed of Christ and the Opposing Spiritual Powers* (GA 107, English translation published under the above title by Steiner Book Centre, Vancouver, Canada, 1976); the answers to questions posed to Rudolf Steiner on 21 April 1909 at Düsseldorf, at the end of a cycle of ten lectures *The Spiritual Hierarchies and their Reflection in the Physical World* (GA 110, English translation published by Anthroposophic Press, New York 1970); and also the last lecture of the cycle, 'The Mysteries of Light, of Space and of the Earth', given in Dornach in December 1919 (GA 194, English translation published under the title of *Ideas for a New Europe*, Rudolf Steiner Press 1992).
15. Ibid.
16. Ibid.
17. Ibid.
18. The bylina 'How the holy mountains released the mighty Russian heroes from their rocky caves' was first published (in Russian) in 1938 under the imprint of 'Prepodobny Iov Pochaesky' (St Job Pochaesky). These and subsequent quotations are taken from Misheyev's foreword.
19. Rudolf Steiner speaks about the spiritual background of the Mongol invasion in the lecture which he gave in Dornach on 17 September 1916 (GA 171, English translation in *Inner Impulses of Human Evolution*, Anthroposophic Press 1984).
20. This lecture is the fourth in the cycle entitled *Polarities in the Evolution of Mankind. West and East. Materialism and Mysticism. Knowledge and Belief.* Cycle of eleven lectures given by Rudolf Steiner in Stuttgart between March and November 1920 (GA 197, English translation published by Rudolf Steiner Press and Anthroposophic Press, 1987).
21. See Rudolf Steiner's lecture-cycle, *The Apocalypse of St John* (see Note 5).
22. See Rudolf Steiner's lecture given on 1 October 1911 in Basel, *The Etherisation of the Blood. The Entry of the Etheric Christ into the Evolution of the Earth* (English translation, Rudolf Steiner Press 1971; also included in *The Reappearance of Christ in the Etheric*, Anthroposophic Press, 1983).
23. See the books by Rudolf Steiner referred to in Note 3.
24. See the lecture given by Rudolf Steiner on 16 November 1917 in St Gallen, *The Mystery of the Double. Geographic Medicine* (GA 178, English translation published by Mercury Press, New York 1979).
25. See the lecture given by Rudolf Steiner on 30 March 1918 (GA 181; an English translation is available from the Library, Rudolf Steiner House, in typescript form: C:49, 'Anthroposophical Life-Gifts').
26. See the lecture given by Rudolf Steiner on 6 January 1914 in Berlin (GA 148; English translation available from the Library, Rudolf Steiner House, in typescript form: R 46, 'On the Fifth Gospel').

27. See Rudolf Steiner's book (*Knowledge of the Higher Worlds: How is it Achieved?* the chapter entitled 'Conditions').

28. See in this connection Rudolf Steiner's teaching—founded upon the results of modern spiritual research—regarding the 'Threefold Social Order', as expounded in his book *The Threefold Social Order* (GA 23) and in many of his articles and lectures. An English rendering of the above book is published by Anthroposophic Press, New York 1972, and by Rudolf Steiner Press under the title *Towards Social Renewal* (1977). The special predisposition of the Russian people for taking up the ideas of the Threefold Social Order is confirmed by, for example, the following words of Rudolf Steiner: '... I know that the Russian people have within them the elements for being the very first to grasp the idea of threefoldness, if it is communicated to them in the right way': from answers to questions posed after the lecture of 25 October 1919 (GA 332a). Regarding the connection between the idea of threefoldness and the Russian village communities, see the lecture of 7 August 1920 (GA 199).

29. A cycle of ten lectures given in April 1912 in Helsinki (GA 136, English translation published by Anthroposophic Press, 1981).

30. See the so-called 'First lecture for Russians', given by Rudolf Steiner in Helsinki on 11 April 1912 (GA 158, not available in English).

31. The 'second lecture for Russians' was given by Rudolf Steiner on 5 June 1913 in Helsinki while he was giving a cycle of nine lectures entitled 'The Occult Significance of the Bhagavad Gita'. An English translation of part of this lecture to Russian members is obtainable from the Library, Rudolf Steiner House (Typescript EN 44).

32. From the lecture given by Rudolf Steiner on 22 March 1909 in Berlin (see Note 14).

33. See the lecture entitled *The Occult Significance of Blood*, given by Rudolf Steiner in Berlin on 25 October 1906 (GA 55, English translation published by Rudolf Steiner Press, 1967).

34. See Note 32.

35. See the third and seventh lectures in Rudolf Steiner's lecture-cycle *The Apocalypse of St John* (see Note 5).

Bibliographical Note

The complete collection of Rudolf Steiner's works has been in process of publication since 1956 in Dornach (Switzerland) in the German language. The edition is being brought out by Rudolf Steiner's literary estate, the 'Rudolf Steiner Nachlassverwaltung'. In all, 354 volumes are planned, the great majority of which are already published. Around fifty of these volumes consist of written works, with approximately 300 volumes of lectures. During the time of his anthroposophical activity Rudolf Steiner gave roughly six thousand lectures throughout Europe, stenographical notes of which are available in the case of the great majority. His principal works, together with his numerous lectures, have been translated into all the major languages of the world; there are also editions in Braille for blind people.

The bibliographical survey that follows is divided into categories in accordance with the catalogue *Rudolf Steiner—Das literarische und künstlerische Werk. Eine bibliographische Übersicht*, Rudolf Steiner Verlag, Dornach, Switzerland 1984. The volume numbers given in this edition appear italicised in brackets; this system of numbering is the one which has now been generally adopted (= Gesamtausgabe number, or GA).

Virtually all of Rudolf Steiner's books and a large proportion of his lectures are available in English translation. Rudolf Steiner Press, Bristol, England and Anthroposophic Press, New York, USA, endeavour to maintain the availability in English of his most important works, and there are similar publishing houses in other English-speaking countries. Typescripts of translations which have not been published, together with copies of the published works, are available from the Library, Rudolf Steiner House, 35 Park Road, London NW1 6XT.

A. Written works

1. *Books*

The Scientific Works of Goethe with Introductions and Commentaries by Rudolf Steiner, 5 vols. 1883–97 (*1*)

A Theory of Knowledge Implicit in Goethe's World Conception, 1886 (*2*)

Truth and Knowledge, 1892 (*3*)

The Philosophy of Freedom, 1894 (*4*)

Friedrich Nietzsche, Fighter for Freedom, 1895 (*5*)

Goethe's World View, 1897 (*6*)

Mysticism at the Dawn of the Modern Age and its Relationship to Modern World-Conceptions, 1901 (*7*)

Christianity as Mystical Fact and the Mysteries of Antiquity, 1902 (*8*)

Theosophy. An Introduction to the Supersensible Knowledge of the World and the Destination of Man, 1904 (*9*)

Knowledge of the Higher Worlds. How is it Achieved? 1904/5 (*10*)

Cosmic Memory, 1904/8 (*11*)

The Stages of Higher Knowledge, 1905/8 (*12*)

Occult Science—An Outline, 1910 (*13*)

The Four Mystery Plays, 1910/13 (*14*)

The Spiritual Guidance of Man and Humanity, 1911 (*15*)

The Calendar of the Soul, 1912 (in *GA 40*)

A Road to Self-knowledge, 1912 (*16*)

The Threshold of the Spiritual World, 1913 (*17*)

The Riddles of Philosophy, 1914 (*18*)

The Riddle of Humanity, 1916 (*20*)

The Riddles of the Soul, 1917 (*21*)

The Mind of Goethe as revealed in his 'Faust' and in the 'Fairy-Tale of the Snake and the Lily', 1918 (*22*)

Basic Issues of the Social Question, 1919 (*23*)

Articles about the Threefold Social Order, 1915–1921 (*24*)

Philosophy, Cosmology and Religion, 1922 (*25*)

Anthroposophical Leading Thoughts. The Anthroposophical Path of Knowledge. The Michael Mystery, 1924/25 (*26*)

The Fundamentals of Therapy, an Extension of the Art of Healing through Spiritual Knowledge, 1925 (*27*): with Ita Wegman

The Course of My Life, 1923/25 (*28*)

II. *Collections of Articles*

Articles on Drama, 1889–1901 (*29*)—Methodical Foundations of Anthroposophy, 1884–1901 (*30*)—Articles on the History of Culture and Contemporary History, 1887–1901 (*31*)—Articles on Literature, 1886–1902 (*32*)—Biographies and Biographical Sketches, 1894–1905 (*33*)—Articles on Philosophy, Anthroposophy etc., 1903–25 (*34–36*)

III. *Publications from the Literary Estate:*
Letters—Verses and dicta—Drafts of the Four Mystery Plays (*38–45*)

B. Lectures

I. *Public Lectures*
Questions of culture, science, spiritual knowledge and Christology in the light of spiritual science (*51–84*)

II. *Lectures for Members of the Anthroposophical Society*
Lectures and cycles of lectures with a general anthroposophical content—Christology and studies of the Gospels—Spiritual-scientific knowledge of man—Cosmic and human history—The spiritual foundations of the social question—Man in his relationship with the cosmos—Karma studies—Esoteric teachings (*93–245*)

Writings and lectures on the history of the anthroposophical movement and the Anthroposophical Society (*254–65*)

III. *Lectures and Courses for Specific Areas of Life*
Lectures on art: Aesthetics—Eurythmy—Speech formation and dramatic art—Architecture—Fine arts—Music—History of art (*271–92*)—Lectures on education (*293–311*)—Lectures on medicine (*312–19*)—Lectures on science (*320–27*)—Lectures on social life and the Threefold Social Order (*328–41*)—Lectures for those working on the building of the Goetheanum (*347–54*)

C. Reproductions and publications from the artistic legacy

Studies for the paintings, sculptures and architectural works of the First Goetheanum—Drawing exercises for artists—Designs for eurythmy productions—Eurythmy forms—Sketches for the eurythmy figures etc.